TALL IN SPIRIT

meditations for the chronically ill

JONI WOELFEL

ASSISTING CHRISTIANS TO ACT
PUBLICATIONS

Tall in Spirit
meditations for the chronically ill
by Joni Woelfel

Editod by Kass Dotterweich
Cover design by Tom A. Wright
Page design and typesetting by Garrison Productions

Published by: ACTA Publications
                Assisting Christians To Act
                4848 N. Clark Street
                Chicago, IL 60640-4711
                773-271-1030

Library of Congress Catalog Number: 99-65634

ISBN: 9-87946-208-6

Printed in the United States of America

99 00 01 02 03 Year/Printing 8 7 6 5 4 3 2 1

Contents

Dedication

This book is dedicated to the memory of Dominic, our dear "Mic," who died too young.

October 30, 1981 – August 7, 1999

Introduction

A few years ago our youngest son went through a frustrating time because he couldn't jump as high as his friends when they had jumping contests; our son was quite a bit shorter than his friends. Being competitive, he decided to find a way to improve the heights he could reach.

One day I heard him pounding and sawing in the garage. "What in the world are you doing?" I asked when I went to check on him. Flabbergasted, I stared at the large blocks of wood that he had nailed and tied onto the soles of an old pair of tennis shoes. Putting these contraptions on his feet, he paraded around on his heels with his toes sticking up, thus stretching the muscles along the back of his calves. Grinning, he said, "It'll stretch my leg muscles and then I'll be able to jump higher." It took him only about two minutes to figure out that his idea just wasn't going work. I went back into the house, laughing to myself.

At the time I thought of the shoes as a symbol that humorously represented the urge we all have to jump high—and the lengths we will go to stretch the necessary muscles to accomplish that. The shoes also symbolized the acceptance of what we can't change, although our son didn't want to go there, of course. He wanted to rush growth and get tall—and that was that! "It will happen," I would tell him. "You'll grow." But in my heart, I wasn't sure. He was pretty short.

For several years he had me mark his height on the wall in my studio so we could chart his growth. I have to admit that I sometimes raised the ruler just a fraction of an inch and exclaimed hopefully, "Oh look, you really are growing!" But we both knew it wasn't true. I would note his worried, disappointed look, but there was nothing I could do. I couldn't make him grow.

Although the waiting took several years, the marks on the wall suddenly started to reach higher levels. We could hardly believe how fast he was shooting up. His grin warmed my heart, and the day came when we stopped measuring altogether.

This book, like the time our son pounded the wooden blocks onto the soles of his tennis shoes, represents my own pounding and sawing out in the garage of my soul: my attempt at making sense of the chronic illnesses I experience. Specifically, I've lived with severe Meniere's disease all my adult life. I also have facial Bell's palsy, a mitral valve prolapse of the heart, and an unusual muscle weakness disorder, lipid storage myopathy, which several specialists think is complicated by chronic fatigue immune dysfunction syndrome. Because of these problems, I have become intimately acquainted with suffering—emotionally and spiritually. Suffering with my chronic illnesses has shaken me by the scruff of the neck so powerfully that I've felt my teeth rattle.

Like our son's growth marks on the wall, these essays symbolize the days of waiting, the in-between time when nothing appeared to be happening—except a lot of inner wrenching due to a body that seemed to be falling apart. Years of enduring adversity passed until one day, almost as suddenly as the onset of our son's growth spurt, I recognized how tall in spirit I had become—and always had been.

When we are tall in spirit, we have the grace to see beyond dark days and dark times, even when we are still in the midst of them. Hope arrives, inner strength grows, and endurance grounds us. We begin to view the unknowns of our lives as an unveiling rather than an unraveling. We learn that there is a rhythm to waiting.

Although it was a long wait, becoming tall was one of the most magical things that ever happened to our son. Becoming tall in spirit is even more wondrous. This book represents my own story of the wonder that carries us even during our darkest times.

The Lock and Key

Some mysteries remain locked to us. Things happen that can't be explained, while the question "Why?" echoes across the canyons deep within.

"Why am I ill? Why can't I get better? Why me? Why not me?" We would be less than human if we did not ask these questions when ongoing suffering gnaws at our very sinews. We are told that everything happens for a reason, but for many, that reason is never revealed.

"Where is the key?" I entreated a confidante one time when another week's worth of physical suffering had me in its grip. "I just need the key," I repeated, imagining a large iron key that would unlock the mysteries of my diseases.

One day, when the longing for that key was more wrenching than usual, I took a walk along a familiar trail. I walked all the way to Red Rock Rapids, where I balanced myself on the stepping stones while the water rushed and gurgled around my feet. Bent over at the waist, I peered into the water, noting minnows, jagged rocks and bits of rippling grass.

Then I noticed something unusual in the water, half covered with furry moss. Slipping my hand into the cool stream, I retrieved what plainly was a lock and key—the key being a dead bolt that was permanently rusted into the lock. The dead bolt and lock had become so melded together, in fact, that it was as if they had become one. I immediately felt a connection with my illness, but I didn't know what it was.

A few days later I had an appointment with a neurologist. After pouring out the long, complicated story, I said, "But I don't want to give up. I want to keep trying." The doctor looked at my file, reviewing an abnormal report from a muscle biopsy he had taken, and said, "These may be all the answers we can give you. We all want to help, but you may have to accept that this is all we can do. Your disease is difficult to understand—even for specialists." I sensed such caring in him that this alone was healing.

"Did you receive any hope?" a friend asked me later that day.

"Not exactly," I said, "but I did receive support." Tears sprang into my eyes, then, as I made the connection: support and hope—like the rusty lock and key that I had found—are sometimes one and the same. I realized that there is no shame in saying, "I can't make it through this by myself."

Healing God of Support and Hope, sometimes we overlook the most powerful answers because we expect something else. Thank you for sending those keys that remind us that there are many ways to experience the mystery of healing.

The Killing Frost

Praise the Lord from the earth...
fire and hail, snow and frost.
Psalm 148:7-8

A cross the road in the horse pasture, several small, bright orange bonfires blinked in the dark where our neighbor was clearing brush. I had watched out the window all evening as the flames diminished to embers that flared when the wind picked up. The novelty of the flames on that black, frigid night was mesmerizing.

The weather reports said that the first killing frost would come that night. I could feel the bite of its approach when I stepped out for a minute to listen to the drone of the combines and corn dryers. As I watched the flames across the road die down and the glowing embers disappear into blackness, I made a note to myself: "Killing frost always wins in the end, doesn't it? Fire and frost are never companions."

There was no light in the pasture for hours—not even a spark. Then suddenly, a fire sprang up, leaping to life for a short time before it died back down to embers. Another thought entered my mind like a wisp of smoke: "There is an ember in each one of us that the killing frost of suffering can't put out, no matter how cold life gets."

I had waited for the killing frost for weeks. Finally it crept into town overnight without a sound. In the morning, when I looked out the window across the yard, the whole world appeared to be covered with a white glaze. Dressed in my long, wool coat, I set off to experience the autumn woods.

The first subtle change I noted was the accelerated rate at which the leaves were falling. Then, as I climbed a bank and stepped out onto a gravel road, I caught sight of a tractor plowing the hillside—a reminder that one season had ended and another was beginning. I knew it would not be long before the black earth furrows would be drifted in with snow.

The reflection of the sun on the rippling water at Philosophy Point was as blinding as it was beautiful—one minute white-gold, the next dripping bronze. I noticed blackened leaves on some of the broad-leafed weeds that stood drooping and dying along the banks, contrasting with the tougher weeds that were seemingly untouched.

It seemed important that I be there on that day, to acknowledge the transformation and to be a part of it. This was a threshold day, when two different seasons come together in an overlapping of time and space. I had been pondering the theology of hope, but as I walked along, such concerns seemed inconsequential. The serenity of that first day after the killing frost was not something I had expected.

I sometimes compare suffering to killing frost; it diminishes us, often harshly, to the bones of the soul. I know, however, that God's foreshadowing envelops all that is, all that is greater than myself, all that is greater than suffering. Like the living stillness that lingers in the woods after that first killing frost, God's foreshadowing wraps itself around us like autumn afternoon sunlight.

God of Changing Seasons, when the season of suffering enters our life and we stand at the threshold of despair, you stir the embers in our soul. We need your warm arms around us when the killing frost of pain makes life cold.

Companions in Hope

There is hope for your future, says the Lord.
Jeremiah 31:17

Years ago, when I made my first trip to a famous clinic, I was innocent, wide-eyed and unseasoned by suffering. I didn't know what to expect, how to act, where to go, or what to think. I was sick and desperate, looking for help in an unfamiliar world. I naively expected a magic pill.

Instead, I found people just like me, from all over the world, seeking hope. Some of these people had memorable spirits that linger in my memory even to this day. The following excerpt is from an old notebook I kept during that time:

Faces stay with you for a long time. Approaching me from the aisle, an elderly gentleman asked politely, "Is this seat taken?" Welcoming the company (as I was quite distressed) I moved my things and smiled, "No, sit down!" We struck up a conversation immediately. He told me that he was a father of seven and a retired farmer who lived in a county not too far from where I lived in southwestern Minnesota.

"Crops are terrible in our area," I said.

"Oh, I know . . . . Here, too. Plowed all the corn under. One more year like this and we'll be done," he explained ruefully.

We sat companionably in silence for a moment. "You a farm girl?" he asked.

"Born and raised," I said, noting his pleased look.

"Your folks still farming?"

I hesitated. "Well, no. They died young."

Sincere sympathy filled his eyes as he said, "My own parents both died in 1943. That was hard to take."

A quiet bond settled between us until my name was called. Rising, I patted his knee and said, "See you later." When I returned, though, he was gone—and I never saw him again, never found out his name. I re-membered his face, however, for a long time.

My next encounter was in a mammogram wait-ing room where six of us women were gathered, attired in incredibly wrinkled, white gowns. A woman sitting next to me quipped, "You'd think they could iron these things." I laughed, liking her on the spot. She made a dry, hilarious comment about the mammogram test (which I can't repeat) while I observed her brilliant coral nail polish and the fact that her whole arm was in a cast. Humor is always part of the coping game, and these women had it down to an art.

Another woman said, "Gee, the test will only take me half the time. I only have one breast left." The woman with the statement nail polish didn't bat an eye when she responded, "Well, you should get a discount then." We all laughed, except for an older woman who sat frozen in fear, not speaking. We were careful not to invade her privacy. All around me, the women were conversing pleasantly, but I noticed that over half were nervously tapping their feet.

Years later I would wonder about the farmer, the nail polish lady, and the woman with one breast. While their faces faded from memory with time, an essence of their good humor lingered like a silver strand. They were the first of many companions in hope whose lives would intersect with mine for brief, significant moments in time. I never dreamed there could be so many of us, all seeking the same thing: hope.

God of Hope against Hope, none of us knows our future. Yet humor can be hope; holding hands can be hope; peace can be hope. Sinking into you is our greatest hope, no matter what happens.

Alligators of Fear

Then you scare me with dreams
and terrify me with visions.

Job 7:14

Fear is a sneaky thing that creeps into our dreams and subconscious without our knowing it. If fear is there in our waking hours, we should not be surprised that it goes to bed with us.

A while ago I dreamed that I was sitting at a desk in a classroom with other students. The classroom was close, crowded and heavily carpeted. Huge lumps started to appear beneath the carpet and roll down the rows between the desks. Everyone fearfully scrambled to lift their feet because alligators were passing through. I remember being afraid that an alligator would break through the carpet and gobble me up.

The scene in the dream then shifted from the classroom to the school bus. All the students had boarded the bus, but I was left behind. I remember running toward the bus as it pulled away, shouting, "Wait!" But I was too late. I missed the bus because someone had stolen my luggage, and my glasses were in the luggage. I kept lamenting, "Not my glasses. I need them to see!"

I began crying, "I can't get through this by myself"—a phrase I've said over and over, like a broken record, in my waking thoughts. I've told my friends repeatedly that I am afraid that I won't handle my illness with the courage and dignity that will make others proud of me.

In my dream that fear manifested itself in reptilian form—as the alligators. Missing the bus represented my ongoing fear of being left behind by life. Having my glasses stolen represented not being able to see the future, feeling as if illness had stolen it from me. Illness had also stolen the dreams and goals I've carried with me for years, represented by the luggage. In the dream I was left empty handed and separated from what I used to take for granted when I had normal health.

I realized that I had been trying to do away with the fear and sense of loss that my illness has entailed, as if those emotions were just something that needed to be worked through and eradicated. Over the years these feelings have become less intense, but ongoing situations and symptoms that create conflict and emotional responses can still bring them to the surface. I have learned to adjust and to develop new goals, even though the process still feels scary. By learning to not be alarmed when fear visits me, I am able to take my nightmares in stride. I have consciously decided that

when the alligators come, I will let them have their say—
and what they say is a message of encouragement:
"Sometimes we just need to be brave."

*Stalwart God of the Ages, even though we want to
and would if we could, we cannot run away from
illness. Teach us to stand firm and face our fear.
Teach us to see it for what it really is—simply an
emotion that is neither good nor bad.*

Stone and Sky

I will keep watch to see what he will say to me....
The very stones will cry out from the wall.

Habakkuk 2:1, 11

Sixteenth floor at a famous clinic. Stone and sky. Crushing chest pain. "I can't go home like this," I said to the kind cardiologist who listened intently, test results spread out across his desk. Behind him, beyond the large window, I saw dark storm clouds contrasted against the imposing watchtower of a nearby complex encompassed with stone gargoyles and guardians. My mind operated on two planes: the present—consisting of anxiety from physical suffering—and an unconscious turning toward the stark, untouchable beauty of stone against sky.

The week rushed by and the days blurred together. When I finally got home my thoughts were muddled. I kept thinking that there was a message woven into the exhaustion, but it kept escaping me. Although I didn't know it, the stone-and-sky message was weaving steadily into my ongoing experience. I could remember glancing at the panoramic view one last time as I prepared to leave at the end of that week, feeling that those pale, sand-colored gargoyles and guardians were trying to remind me of something. I simply couldn't figure out what.

For some inexplicable reason, the stone-and-sky impression continued to haunt me. I would find myself frowning and staring out the window, feeling the tug of a message that wouldn't surface. Then one night, as I was reflecting in the twilight that comes right before sleep, a memory slipped through. I was ten years old. A storm was brewing and its refreshing gusts brushed pleasantly across my sweaty face after a hot day. I was down by the barn where I had just taken an icy drink from the pump spigot. Standing by the wooden water tank, I gazed at the big hill beyond the pasture and enjoyed the cooling wind billowing beneath my cotton shirt. The cured, wheat-colored grass rolled in waves, responding to the wind as if a mighty hand were passing through it. The color of the brooding, gunmetal blue of the stormy sky against the pale grass that swelled like a sea was breathtaking. It was as if the world consisted of only hill and sky. A mysterious, profound sense of well being enveloped me which, as a child, I took at face value, letting the experience drift gently into that inner place where I kept things.

Gradually I realized that the stone-and-sky impression had been tugging at me because of the parallel to that childhood memory. The colors, the ambience and the feelings were the same. Both the stone-and-sky impression and that childhood memory were powerful, touchstone images that evoked an inner truth I have always known but had forgotten: there is a secret nerve that answers to the call of beauty. While this is a unique and spiritual experience for each person, one thing is clear: within that response lies light, inner strength and renewal. When I think of the thousands of people who have come and gone under the watchful eyes of the clinic's stone guardians, I can only wonder, did the image of stone against sky touch them? Did they understand the message?

God of Stone and Sky, your message to us is simple: "No matter what happens, I am with you. You will be all right."

Flower Beds and Family Love

Those who till their land will have plenty.
Proverbs 12:11

One spring day our middle son, home from college, cleaned out my flowerbeds. I watched as he cleaned away the old growth from the newly sprouting plants. My son's hands were caked with dirt, and he had that light in his eyes that he gets when he is working with the earth.

I have planned and worked on our flowerbed designs, which have grown with our family for nearly twenty-five years. They are like my own thumbprint, a part of me and who I am. But that particular day I tired quickly and turned to go back into the house, leaving my son to work alone. "It's hard for me not to be able to do that anymore," I said.

"I was wondering about that," my son replied knowingly, protective of me and insightful as always.

Sometimes I blame myself because my illness keeps me from being there for my family the way I should be—the way I want to be. It has been difficult for me not to whitewash the truth of the toll that my struggle has taken on all of us, both individually and collectively. Living the myth of the perfect, all-American family is strong in me. Yet one of the wisest and hardest things I've had to learn in coping with my illness is to let go of my illusions.

My family and I don't have to express all the details about the difficulties of living with my illness, but we do need to see and face the truth. Until we do that, we can't begin to move on and be there for one another in ways that are real and forgiving.

Please, Parent God, help my family be watchful and present to one another's comings and goings and passages. Remind us that illness is but another part of our family's reality and love.

Snakeskin Shoes and Pink Refrigerators

Ah, you are beautiful, my beloved,
truly lovely.

Song of Solomon 1:16

Giving up being able to wear high heels as a result of my diseases caused me a lot of grief at first, because heels were something that made me feel attractive and womanly. I now wear thick-cushioned tennis shoes, and I often carry a cane.

At first I felt painfully self-conscious, especially when I caught people staring at me. Once, dressed in a long navy blue wool coat, I asked my husband, "Don't I look rather mysterious and dignified?" I remember feeling quite satisfied with myself at the time, thinking, "This isn't so hard. I can do this." Before long, however, I had another serious challenge to get used to.

Following surgical complications, I was left with permanent paralysis on the left side of my face. When I looked in the mirror for the first time, I was horrified to see that half of my face looked like it had melted. To make things worse, I had to have my eye surgically sewed half shut. I made it through those dark, frightening months, but as they passed, the paralysis and muscle weakness did not. I no longer looked or even felt like myself.

One day I got rid of my high-heel shoes, but I couldn't part with a favorite pair of snakeskin heels that I'd worn only once. I remember lingering prayerfully over them as I knelt in the dark closet and gently placed them in a box. My eyes were dry but my heart was weeping with the letting go of the person I used to be.

Later I cut out of a magazine a funny photo depicting a woman dressed in flamboyant pink—an advertisement for some new, scented, pink garbage bags. I chuckled at the woman's hair—done in an exaggerated, outrageous style—and her pink refrigerator. I scrawled across the bottom of the photo: "If one can't be beautiful, go for flair!" I was beginning the process of not taking my looks so seriously but rather basing my self-worth on dimensions beneath the skin.

When I was going through the worst of the adjustment, I received a letter from my surgeon. He said, "It is quite true that all of us need to have an inner spirit and strength in order to sustain us through the difficulties of life. Anytime a person has a problem because they have 'no shoes,' I refer to another who has 'no feet.' There are many reasons for each of us to count our blessings." He concluded by offering ongoing support, saying that while there is not always a cure for a problem, there is always help and hope.

I clung to those words. They, along with the snakeskin shoes and the photo of the funny pink woman with weird hair and a pink refrigerator, became touchstones in my inner memory book. I wrote in my journal: "Humor and beauty wrought through suffering are of the bravest, most sacred kind. It only stands to reason that those who make this rite of passage should paint their refrigerators pink, don't you think?" I was so glad that even though my ability to recognize these truths of the heart seemed small, I was able to do it—at least a little.

God of Many Faces, when inner beauty is awakened, it is like a light coming on in the soul. The irony is that we would never go back to our old "looks" if it would mean giving up the deepening sense of self we come to experience.

Things I Forgot

They forgot what he had done,
and the miracles that he had shown them.

Psalm 78:11

I went for a short walk one winter night after spending the weekend in bed, once again, due to incapacitating vertigo. As I walked, I felt "out of sync," unable to get with the rhythm of things. It was as if my soul needed adjusting, as our eyes do when we're first plunged into darkness. I felt myself making up a mental list I called my "I Forgot List" that helped me reclaim my balance.

I forgot how much I love wearing my long, wool coat with my favorite rhinestone pin.

I forgot how warm my hands feel in my stretchy gloves grasping my grandfather's cane.

I forgot how much I like the sting of cold cheeks from the biting winter air.

I forgot how beautifully our primitive, outdoor angel banner flutters as it catches the wind.

I forgot how the sound of the wind echoing through the empty elevator grain bins pleases me.

I forgot how much I marvel at how tall the row of guardian cottonwoods has grown.

I forgot how dazzling the patchwork of ice crystals in the road ruts looks by moonlight.

I forgot how drawn I am to the winter moon as it etches the white barn on the hill.

I forgot how striking a white horse looks by white moonlight.

I forgot how much I love white.

I forgot how funny, pushy and greedy a horse can be, nosing for apples and sugar.

I forgot how friendly the cracked sidewalk uptown is.

I forgot how much I enjoy slowly spinning the children's merry-go-round in the park.

I forgot how the distant laughter of our village children is infused with a celestial melody.

I forgot how pleasant it is to walk in old, familiar surroundings, knowing every distant yard light and dog bark.

I forgot how truly dark and soul-filling the cover of night can be.

Dear Mindful God, who never forgets a cat paw print in the snow, we forget...we forget. We forget to take notice of all the magical things that are sacred. We would like to say that we will remember to change, but you know only too well that by tomorrow we will probably be as mindless as snow fleas. You'll have to remind us all over again, for which we thank you in advance!

A Small Soft Click

Listen! my beloved is knocking.
Song of Solomon 5:2

Sometimes, when you open a door slowly and carefully, just a crack, you can hear a small click as the
lock mechanism lets go. Click. Soft sound. The door
creaks open. Seeing small truths of the soul can be like
that. There's that small click and a thought comes to us,
revealed through the light of the inner door that has
opened. Sometimes it can be a painful truth that we
have to face, yet we feel a certain sense of freedom or
relief when we do.

As my illnesses progressed, there were times
when I couldn't even handle an hour's conversation
with my friends. Symptoms escalated, reducing my
ability not only to laugh and converse but to listen
properly and respond. At first, my friends said, "Maybe
we shouldn't come anymore. It's too hard on you." They
would never admit it, but I suspect that they felt sorry for
me.

Sometimes I felt as if I just couldn't tolerate not
being on an equal communication footing with my

friends, not having the stamina for hearty discussions on favorite topics. In fact, there were times when I felt I had failed my friends, although I knew they would never want me to think that. I actually wanted to run down the long, dark hallway within myself, weeping about it. I felt so insecure about what I had to offer. Would I ever be able to make peace with the limitations I faced?

I wrote page after page in my journal, wailing my way through my feelings of loss until, finally, there were no words left to write; I'd written them all. I was tired of repeating myself. When I reached the end of myself, however, a quiet stillness stole over me. As I listened to the quiet, without thinking, I wrote, "I think God is knocking."

Then, using my imagination, I heard an inner voice say, "Joni, you're going to have to make peace with this regret thing." It was like an inner door opening with a small, soft click. I realized that my heartache was holding me back and that if I didn't step out of the long, dark hallway, I wouldn't be myself—whatever that might be—for my friends.

As I worked with the regret and faced the fact that I needed to make a change, alternative ways to "be myself" began evolving. I wrote letters to my friends, decorating them with hearts and "smiley" stickers, as my way of not only sharing but caring. I began lighting candles for my friends and making prayer visits to the Great Grandmother trees in the woods behind our house on their behalf. I sent them flowers and small gifts, collected rocks and feathers for them, kept our favorite wine coolers and herbal teas on hand, and created a gathering space for us in a loft overlooking stained-glass windows in my home.

It took time, but as I began adjusting to my limitations, relaxing and healing from the wrenching of my frustrations, I found joy again at being able to feel that I am an important part of my friends' lives.

None of this was easy, of course; I still wish that I was well. Nevertheless, I now know that when I sense a familiar small, soft click, God is encouraging me to step out of my hallway into a new place. Sometimes I can even hear the door creak open.

Oh God of Inner Doorways, sometimes you have to knock a long time before we hear you in our heart. Each doorway we step through has you on both sides. Why does it take us so long to figure that out?

Secret Rhythms

But we speak God's wisdom, secret and hidden.

1 Corinthians 2:7

One day, as our youngest son chatted with me while I rested, I happened to glance out the sliding glass door. "Look at that," I exclaimed. "The trees are moving and there's no wind!"

He turned to look and said, "Oh, it's just pressure."

"Can't you think of something more magical than that?" I teased.

"Well," he said, thinking a minute and grinning, "it's from birds flying by."

Every time I looked out the window that day, I could sense a slight swaying of the trees that border the woods before the landscape drops into the valley. Yet there was no wind except for an occasional wisp that shuttled a solitary, curled leaf to the snow below.

The subtle shifting of the trees reminded me of a childhood game called Freeze. Everyone mills around until someone shouts, "Stop!" Then the children freeze to the spot and become like statues—except, of course, there is always a subtle shifting of limbs because children can never be truly still. There is a magical rhythm within them that keeps time with secret sonatas.

That day was a lost one for me. Symptoms escalated, causing anxiety. It was only later that night, as I sat under an old lap quilt listening to the clock tick, that I felt the stillness of an inner rhythm soothe me, as it always does. Our son was tucked into bed, and I could hear him singing those beautiful, tuneless songs he made up since he was little. I had chanted the blessing song over him and had made the sign of the cross on both him and the cat. He had said hopefully (because he wanted to get out of school), "There's supposed to be a storm front moving in." Then, without missing a cue, he quipped, "I wonder what happens if a storm back moves in?" I laughed, "Don't grow up, don't get any taller, and never leave your room! That way I can keep you safe and sound forever." "Okay," he said, "except I have to get taller." Getting taller was his main goal in life.

Life was always magical to my son. I was like that when I was his age and could have given him a run for his money on who could climb a tree faster. Now I am rediscovering that same magic in a new way through the framework of my illness. It's not about rediscovering lost youth so much as tapping into that life-giving secret rhythm—the kind that makes trees sway when there's no wind.

Enchanting God of Trees That Sway When There's No Wind, no matter how old or sick we become, never let us lose touch with the magic language known only to children.

Rafts and Battleships

He is a shield...
the way of a ship on high seas.
Proverbs 30:5, 19

When I was a child I had a favorite game I used to play. I would place four kitchen chairs in the middle of the living room, front seat to front seat, creating a small platform "raft" that I could sit on. After gathering several pillows and a blanket, my favorite storybooks, like *Frosty the Snowman,* and a jar of dill pickles, the game would begin.

I would pretend that the raft was adrift in the ocean and that sharks invaded the waters. I usually persuaded my sister to sit on the raft with me, because if you're going to be shipwrecked at sea, you definitely want a companion. We couldn't let our legs dangle over the edge of the raft, of course, because the sharks would bite us. Sometimes I would write a secret message to be set adrift so that rescuers would learn of our plight and save us. I would then become known as a heroine—the girl who braved the ocean and won!

As an adult, I did not expect to be living with the

challenges I face regarding illness. I have felt tossed about in an ocean of uncertainty, adrift among sharks patrolling beneath like shadows. So often I have wanted to send out a secret message in a bottle that says, "Urgent! Woman lost at sea. Rescue at once!" I have tried to keep a light-hearted perspective, tried to be funny, but it often sounds phony even to my ears—because it is. I am not laughing. In fact, I often feel strung out and consumed with a profound sense of powerlessness. Even though I know that learning how to develop a personal sense of control is paramount, it often seems like a big joke.

One of the most heartbreaking things I have had to learn is to decide with whom I share my feelings. Sometimes I would say too much; other times, not enough. The stress of feeling that I had to tiptoe around or camouflage the depth of my feelings regarding my illness took a huge emotional toll on me. It was damaging in many ways.

It took me several years to figure it out. When I wrote the following thoughts, I was not being quite true to myself. I wrote:

Those of us who live with chronic illness can't control its tides; we have the power, however, to shape the raft we travel on, carrying our faith, hope and endurance. When people drive by on a cool evening and see me leaning against the railing of my lovely handicap ramp and gazing into the flowerbed below, they have no idea that I am really on the deck of a great ship, peering into the ocean.

Much later, when I came into a fuller understanding, I chided myself saying, "For God's sake, tell the truth; it's a battleship, you fool." I smiled. Expressing the truth will do that to you.

Wholesome God and Ship of Truest Feelings, while some things are best left unsaid, we can pour out the deepest deep to you. You are the one who enfolds us and wants to hear when we need to cry, "Suffering stinks!"

Safe or Unsafe

God...made my way safe.
Psalm 18:32

Both my parents died at young ages, and my sisters and brother and I were intimately involved in their journeys with colon cancer. As I come to terms with the emotional responses I have to my own illnesses, I look back on those experiences from an entirely different perspective. I have a quote on my bulletin board that reads, "Emotion is not inferior or second rate; emotion is a highly valid phase of humanity." I remember those words when I wrestle with vulnerable, needy feelings.

Early on, I tried to view the unknown aspects of this illness-journey as an unveiling instead of an unraveling, because "unveiling" seemed to lend a spirit of ongoing mystery to the journey. I instinctively knew that if I were to have any peace, I would need to understand the rhythms of my illness. Gradually, suffering felt less scary and useless to me when I began to see that the mystery of what I was going through would not destroy me—that I could actually find sacred and even funny moments within it.

During a particularly bad time, when the symptoms had escalated to a point where I had to spend a lot of time in bed, I started feeling alone and wrung out like a rag. Finally, I wrote down every single lamentation that my heart could cry, and then I read the long list to a counselor friend. At the time, it was important to me that someone know exactly what I was feeling. My friend, a good sport, listened respectfully while I read my litany of lamentations. Then, with a twinkle in his eye, he said, "I think that if I were you, I would just stay in bed and take handfuls of Valium all day." I couldn't help but laugh. Having a friend who is willing to wait with me and mindfully take in what I say brought the reassurance I needed to feel secure again.

Will I be safe from the cancer that runs in my family? Will I be able to endure the illnesses I face? These questions settle into the background as I learn to live in the present. As an old favorite quote of mine goes, "You can't change the past, but you can ruin a perfectly good present by worrying about the future." It is incredibly tough at times, but I find my way by sinking into the height, weight and depth of the daily journey.

God of Safe Passages, each day has enough worries and wonders of its own to fill a lifetime. When we allow ourselves to be overwhelmed by alarming things that could happen but rarely do, we paddle right out of your safe thoroughfare into our own imagined harbors of terror. How foolish of us.

Laid Aside: Never

Where there is no guidance, a nation falls,
but in an abundance of counselors there
is safety.

Proverbs 11:14

Years ago my husband and I took a brief excursion to a wonderful, historic town. I remember gazing up at gargoyles on red stone buildings draped against the backdrop of a perfect summer sky. I remember, too, the interesting shops and all the tourists. I also remember being so weak that I could walk only half a block before I needed to sit down and rest.

I was sure time would bring an end to the problem, but a summer later found me with no improvement. I decided to begin working with a clinical social worker who could help me sort out the emotional aspects of my physical illness. Even though I was timid at first, I found being in therapy to be one of the smartest things I've ever done. When we wrote out my evaluation sheet, my therapist noted:

Strengths: passion for living.

What can't be controlled or changed: present

symptoms and what people think.

Goals: for patient to feel less vulnerable and traumatized by suffering, and to address caretaker issues.

Exploration: into the unknown regarding physical weakness and response.

This assessment seemed accurate; it represented a concrete, emotional framework that I could understand and work within. It would take a great deal of doggedness, of course, to keep looking and believing that I could find new ways to make sense of my predicament. It was an important issue with me, however, because for the first time in my life I was beginning to feel useless. Having a counselor I could trust and count on to be a partner in the exploring I needed to do proved to be crucial.

Perhaps the most appealing and dangerous element of chronic illness is the temptation to drop out, to quit trying to rise above or find spiritual meaning in the pain. That summer the theme that stuck in my mind was, "I am not laid aside." My kind counselor reminded me many times that I had my own inner journey to attend to, a journey that would require active participation and responsibility. Sometimes, when I longed to be out in the flowerbeds, riding my old bike, back at work at the post office, hiking in the woods, or playing badminton with my sons, I would say to myself, "I am not laid aside." Yes, I knew this journey to be mine and that I would have to attend to it with active participation and responsibility—but I also knew God's wondrous presence in the compassion and wisdom of my counselor.

Thank you, Faithful God, for sending us those people who remind us that you never "lay aside" anyone. Never.

Lessons from the Desert Fathers and Mothers

In the scrub of the desert plain you will lodge.
Isaiah 21:13

L iving with chronic illness presents an ongoing and unique spiritual challenge. It takes a certain amount of courage to walk the walk as days turn into months and even years. The voice of temptation to give up when the map seems impossible to fathom can catch one unaware, sidling in through the cracks of doubt.

It has come as a great curiosity to me that if I am to cope, I must live in a world of constant redefining. When I read a book about the desert monks, I made a connection to my journey: I understood that the hermits' way of life is only a framework, a kind of scaffolding on which they build the spiritual structure of their lives with God.

Perhaps one of the most important issues I've faced comes from the phrase, "to keep your heart safe." When physical symptoms of chronic illness escalate to levels that are hard to tolerate, the sense of isolation and the unknown can be strong. Thomas

Merton describes the hermit's life as uncharted, like a pioneer with no map. That concept perfectly parallels the journey of chronic illness. I never know from day to day how wild or tame my symptoms will be, and this uncertainty creates understandable confusion. When symptoms are severe I have not been beyond contemplating, "What will become of me?" While this is an acceptable and valid human response to the moment, it is not where I want my thoughts to stay.

In fact, the desert fathers and mothers warn against prolonged thoughts such as these, saying that the dangers of isolation of the self can lead to self-absorption, comparison, the inability to go out of oneself to others, and the incapacity for any form of self-transcendence. They describe this as being a prisoner of one's own selfhood, which is a horrifying thought.

This is one of the greatest dangers the chronically ill face, because of the isolating nature of suffering. No one wants to become mired in repetitious thoughts that go nowhere and bring no growth or light. The desert fathers and mothers exemplify the attitude that aloneness can pave the way for purity of heart, sensibility and—perhaps most importantly—growth in the understanding of (and compassion toward) human frailty. The simple men and women who lived their lives out among the rocks and sands did so only because they entered the desert to be their true selves in God.

The stories of the desert fathers and mothers

renew my conviction that the inner world within the scaffolding of our life circumstances is of the utmost importance. I can think of no greater personal grief for anyone than to look back on life only to discover that there was an outer framework with nothing inside. For that very reason, we must never give up...no matter how much we must redefine our maps.

God of True Hermits and Contemplatives, the desert is not always a forsaken place. Rather, it can be a place of hallowed ground where the soul is filled, not stripped.

Diamonds for Toads

O afflicted one, storm-tossed, and not
*   comforted,*
I am about to set your stones in antimony,
and lay your foundations with sapphires.
I will make...your wall of precious stones.

Isaiah 54:11-12

One magic day I woke up feeling strong enough to work on the computer all morning, mow the lawn in the afternoon, and then wash two loads of laundry. In fact, it was the best day I'd had in a long time. Because it is unusual for me to have such physical strength and stamina, I took the day at face value; I enjoyed and used the gift of every minute.

The best part of the day was mowing the lawn—feeling the breeze ruffle across my face and the sun warm my arms. Frankly, I never thought I would be able to mow the lawn again. The simple pleasure of doing it was extremely satisfying as I looked out over an expanse of lawn that I had mowed by myself.

Only those who suffer from illness will understand what I am about to say: part of me was mad. I was angry because of the unpredictability that chronic illness entails and how it plays with your emotions, never allowing you to define your life or future. You can feel extremely sick and weak one day, and considerably better the next. To me, this is where the cruelty comes in. The good day I had was pure gift, and I was grateful for it. But the next day I was back to using my cane— too weak to do much more than pour the cat a bowl of milk. Who can make sense of a pendulum like that?

Serious illness can be cruel, but the blessings it brings can be significant. I wrote to a friend about this. "It is the most amazing thing," I said, "almost like a spiritual phenomena. The more I experience suffering, the more richness and blessing I seem to experience, almost like it is in direct relation to the pain." I was referring to new friends, insights, an inner knowing, and a marvelous sense of dry humor. I couldn't explain, but I knew that each of these was a white gift springing from black grace—or to use my favorite expression, like a diamond for each toad.

Years later, I received a letter from a friend who, like me, lives with debilitating chronic illness. After a particularly trying time, she wrote, "People do not realize how totally exhausted I get. I feel like running away to a haven, but I don't have one. I am mentally exhausted as well. You have spirit, but I am losing mine— as well as hope. Losing independence is frightening."

My friend's letter touched me deeply. When I was in the worst of it, I did not have a haven either, until

I found one within—and even then, in tough times, I would feel that I was falling apart.

My friend's letter continued: "All my life I have tried to find answers to the meaning of life, read so many how-to books...but they always left me searching for more. There was a void. When I read your thoughts, there is fullness and peace that comes to me."

I smiled when I read her words, because I knew I was a diamond in her life—but only the first of many to come. I wanted to say to her: "But friend, you are a diamond to me."

When life is full of toads, that's how it works. I am glad, so very glad, that the law of the universe weaves a blessing for every cruelty. Later, when I wrote back to my friend, I addressed her as Diamond Woman.

God of Precious Jewels and Toads, when all we can see are warts, you see the potential for diamonds. I really admire that about you, God.

Breath of the Night

He himself gives...life and breath.... "In him we
live and move and have our being."

Acts 17:25, 28

I have always taken midnight walks. I like the privacy at
that time of night and the sense of spirit-healing that
I feel. One summer day, I had been able to emotionally
detach myself, not allowing myself to take my feelings
too seriously, even though I was quite ill. I was learning
to adjust to the chronic emotions that accompany
chronic illness. This process included reining in feelings
that drained me, but I was finding it to be a delicate
balancing act. On the one hand, I needed to feel and
express myself passionately, to let the heat of suffering
rise and find release. On the other hand, I needed to
cool down and learn when not to engage emotion but
rather to allow my response to suffering to settle into
quiet, shadowed healing places.

That night when I went for a walk with our dog,
the wind felt alive, whooshing through the trees with a
loud rushing sound. I could feel it pause, inhaling and
exhaling against my skin with a rhythm like someone
breathing. It played with the ends of my silk scarf and

lifted the unruly fur on our golden retriever's neck. The night bugs were out, and I smiled at the moths flitting softly around the garage light. As I passed the stout, fully-grown stalks of corn that our son had planted by the deck, I could see the green fronds twisting in the wind and brushing the railing of the deck like fingertips. The ears of the corn hung mature and ripe, with beards of brown silk.

The weather was changing; I'd felt it all day. Even though the night was close, warm and uncomfortably damp, there was a feline coolness curling around the mailbox and crouching in the ditches. While the coolness was as invisible as the wind and night voices, I could feel it prickle the length of my bare arms. I paused with my hands on my hips, taken in by the cold, milky, white eye of the moon that peered through a gauze of racing, navy clouds.

Then suddenly, the wind died down, leaving a heavy, flat feeling as my shadow streaked across the road before me. The crunch of my thongs on the gravel sounded louder than before, as if in a void. From the woods, I could hear the fragile, far-away screeching sound of a night creature—a sound that couldn't be heard without the stillness. I likened the experience to the inner voices that the quiet of illness brings, whispering words of encouragement that are as subtle and life-giving as breath itself. The memory of that night settled into my quiet, shadowed healing place, from where I have drawn upon its message many times.

God of Living Stillness, when we feel thrust into a void of suffering, even when we can't find you and feel all alone, your very breath brushes across our lives. This is your gentle caress, your way of saying, "There, there. All will be well."

Backbone of the Soul

I will be with you; I will not fail or forsake you.
Joshua 1:5

I was lying on a massage table with my warm, woolen serape draped over me while the therapist gently worked. Eyes closed, I kept dropping into some secret place within myself. A few pesky flies, however, kept alighting on me, interrupting the rhythm of meditation. I kept thinking of the drone of flies from a childhood summertime memory, letting it carry me back to our green porch on the farm where I used to sit soaking up the sun with Old Gray Mother Cat.

As she worked, the therapist said softly, "You are not abandoned." I had, in fact, been thinking those very words. But when she said them, I thought, "Yes, I am. I am abandoned."

When I still felt that way the next day, I asked myself, "Who or what do you feel has abandoned you?" The answer came immediately: normalcy. Double vision and escalated muscle weakness had kept me in bed yet another day. I said to life, "I can't believe you have abandoned me like this." It was a concept I was working through, a common one among those who are chronically ill.

Let me tell you a story I've never told anyone. There is a small stand of woods in a valley just below our house. Although it's rather scrubby, hardly what people would consider scenic, the spirit of place is strong there. I have become intimately acquainted with its shallow creek, trees and paths, so much so that I made wooden signs for each of them. I began by making a sign for a seldom-used trail; I named it A Path Untrod. I then progressed with signs for places like Philosophy Point, Dead Tree Gulch, Sit-a-Spell Log, and Coon Paw Curve. At Red Rock Rapids there is a grove of six giant trees; I named them the Great Grandmothers.

One day, as I was running along the path to get to Sugar Beach, I came up short and stopped in my tracks. One of the Great Grandmother trees had fallen during the night and lay across the creek, from bank to bank. I could see the base of her large roots broken open to the daylight, red sap, like blood, trickling down onto the white sand. It was like a death, and I felt like weeping.

I've never told anyone about this experience, because I was afraid the sacredness of my feelings would be diminished. The sense of grief stayed with me that entire summer.

Gradually, the bark weathered off the Great Grandmother tree, as she became a natural bridge that spanned the creek for nearly four years. My husband, sons, and I would perch upon her solid bulk and watch the tumbling water below. Eventually, however, floodwaters swept the tree onto the bank, where we still honor her.

The true spirit of the woods is strongest in the fall, when the frost kills the swarms of mosquitoes and the leaves and weeds wither and die. The summer denseness passes away and the backbone of the land is revealed, as it is each fall before the snows come.

The disease I have is like a frost that kills and strips—revealing the backbone of my soul. Perhaps to me, the downed Great Grandmother tree represents the backbone of the woods—skeletal, with only her essence remaining. She speaks to me of a strength and wisdom beyond the physical. She teaches me that change and diminishment are nothing to fear but are, rather, part of a natural process overshadowed by the care of God.

When the fall rains come, and the sky becomes gunmetal gray, and the newly bare branches of the naked trees intertwine in the roaring wind, I think of liturgy. My sacred places in the woods remind me that God does not pass through our lives but rather dwells as a real presence, reminding us that we are never abandoned.

O Tenderhearted God of Fallen Trees and Bare-Branched People, linger long and close.

A Day of Reckoning

You show me the path of life.
Psalm 16:11

We all experience seasons of hardship and, in the process of muddled pain and struggle, an inner transformation begins taking place. One of my reckoning days took place in my beloved woods. After being in the hospital and recovering slowly at home, I had not "seen the world" in many weeks. I was an empty vessel: ill, discouraged, and at odds with myself and the world around me. I felt like my soul was barely breathing.

Finally, alone and weak, I took my deceased grandfather's polished oak cane in hand and headed into the woods, where I hoped to find myself again. Snicker, our neighbor's dog (who looks like a fox) ran to greet me, jumping all over my coat as he always does. I grinned for the first time in weeks. Deer and rabbits had kept my paths open, and I slowly made my way, drinking in the spirit of the woods. I felt a sense of wonder, as if I was seeing the familiar sights for the first time.

I slid down the steep bank—past the Great Grandmother trees that guard the entrance, past my hand-painted sign that reads A Path Untrod—and followed the footprints of the deer. Sheltering tree branches bent low in front of me, laden with the weight of heavy snow. In many places I had to duck under the supple canopy while snow sprinkled down my neck. I paused at Little Fellow's Fishing Hole, reflecting on how incredibly fast the summer had passed through a blur of illness. It had been a long time, too long, since I had visited the woods. It made me feel sad to be a stranger in a place where I had always felt a strong sense of my roots—more so than any other place.

As I headed into the darker, more hidden and mysterious part of the woods, I sensed a presence; I was not alone. A large, tawny doe watched me from the thicket on a nearby hill, moving silently and ghost-like along the bank. Although she suddenly disappeared from sight, I knew she wasn't far away and was following my every move. At that moment I felt a heightened curiosity and a sense of sacredness toward all of life.

As I headed back along the snow-packed path, past Deer Hideout, I found a bloody deer hoof print, crimson against the white snow. Knowing it was hunting season, I trudged on, sobered and thoughtful of the complexities of our world.

Retracing my steps, poking along with my cane, the spirit of the woods continued to nourish me, bringing me inner peace, renewal, and a keen sense of wonder at the beauty of the world. As I stepped out onto the gravel road, symbolic of the journey still ahead of me, I greeted myself. I was back.

Sometimes we forget, Gentle God, that there is a path of life just waiting for us to tread. Although we tremble from the exertion of physical and emotional struggle, our soul breathes in all the sacred wonders of your world.

Prayerful Howling

I cry for help until morning;
like a lion he breaks all my bones.

Isaiah 38:13

Years ago horrendous floods wiped out all of my woodland trails, leaving only the central backbone path. All the wooden trail signs I had painted were swept away, except for a remnant here and there left lying on the ground with nails sticking out. I grieved deeply.

With time, of course, the denseness of the woods returned to its natural, nearly impenetrable state. It was as if the woods reclaimed itself, becoming once again a wild, untamed place. The very creek itself changed course, gouging out the far side of the railroad trestle bank and retreating from the old beach that we used to know. The felled Great Grandmother tree lay crooked and abandoned, half out of the water, no longer providing a natural bridge. All these landscape changes took place in a few short years. The voraciousness and continuity of change in the woods awed me, yet I felt attuned to it somehow.

The illness that has physically diminished me has also ravaged my inner landscape, changing me as drastically as the woods have been changed by the floodwaters. A transformation has been taking place in my soul, gouging out whole banks where waters once ran deep, over-running tame places, and flooding my inner terrain. Many of my old and familiar inner paths have been washed out by the raging waters of chronic illness. I don't know precisely at what point I began recognizing this inner wildness. I think I felt it happening long before I understood what it was.

Sometimes, when the illness is severe, I feel a wildness in me that defies description, like a wolf that has been stuck in a cage and is howling to get out. The closest I can come to explaining this is to say that it is like prayer that comes from the deepest deep—wild and passionate for life and freedom.

There is nothing soft or gentle about long-term, serious illness. Its force has the power to ravage like raging floodwaters, and its bite is like that of a caged animal. It has driven me wild, in the sacred sense of the word. Sometimes I think it is this wildness that will save me. A tame woman could never howl...and this journey requires howling in the most prayerful, ferocious sense.

Oh God of All That Howls, the brutality of suffering defies words. Sometimes we can't even pray about it. It's not that we don't want to. It's just that our soul is too busy growling with the pain and horror. Still the floodwaters, God; still the beast.

Bone Woman

"Can these bones live?" I answered, "O Lord God, you know."

Ezekiel 37:3

B one Woman—the only grotesque thing in our house—resides behind glass in a cabinet in our living room. If you examine her closely, you will see that she is a statue—about one and a half feet tall—of disintegrating plaster. Bone Woman wears a green moss-covered skirt, and on her back she carries a basket—now broken in half and encrusted with black earth. She is bent over in a hag-like pose, and her face is so corroded that it looks skeletal. The plaster she is crafted from is so weathered that it is porous and full of holes, resembling bone.

I found Bone Woman lying discarded in the woods one week when I had been near my wits' end with suffering, feeling reduced to the bones of my soul. Spiritually, I felt cold, skeletal and alone. I had railed at God, "I can only take so much. You've got to come through for me in a way that I can understand."

When I found her, I felt an immediate connection to Bone Woman, and I brought her home with me. It took nearly a week for the plaster to dry but, even then, pieces of it brushed off like grains of sand when touched. While fragile in the physical sense, Bone Woman nonetheless gives an impression of strength and knowing.

After some thought, I was able to put her story together. Over fifteen years ago, I had purchased the statue to serve as an outdoor ornament. She was a lovely maiden back then, European in style, with beautiful detail. I planted petunias in her basket one season, but she did not weather well. The basket broke and, somehow, Bone Woman got thrown out. She lay hidden in the woods all these years, completely transformed, only to be discovered by me when I needed her.

The silence of her transformation is awesome. Resting in the dark shadows of the woods, autumn leaves covered her, winter snowstorms buried her, spring rains beat upon her, and summer insects scurried across her. As time passed, she sank into the earth, where dampness penetrated to her core, defleshing her to where she is no longer recognizable as a lovely maiden. I think that I could actually weep at what she has gone through, but I understand the spirit, strength and wisdom that she represents—the holy work of coming into fullness through deepening and diminishment.

Bone Woman looks as old as time itself. It seems to me that it would be a sacrilege to try to clean her up in any way. She speaks to me of paradox at its most beautiful, embracing level.

Oh God Who Breathes Life into All Living Things, the Bone Woman in each of us longs for your spirit. You are her loyal heart, deep listener, life force. You are keeper of our deepest deep, guardian of the fragile bones of the soul.

When the Heart Weeps

Weeping may linger for the night,
but joy comes with the morning.
Psalm 30:5

Ongoing suffering shapes our lives and influences the framework in which we define and express our faith, our relationships, and who we are. Serious chronic illness affects how we live our lives to the marrow of our beings.

Once, while doing some meditation work with a close friend, I confided that sometimes, when I am really sick, I feel like sobbing. She asked, "Do you tell anyone?" Without thinking, I blurted out the strangest thing: "No, it's not marketable." She said, "Forget marketing (actually, she used stronger language than that)! When you need to sob, you should sob."

I had unconsciously taken on the prevailing attitude that during long-term suffering, crying on a regular basis is unacceptable. People expect it when we are first diagnosed with cancer, for instance, or when a loved one dies. But before long, we are expected to "get over it," which leaves us feeling like our tears are somehow less acceptable.

When suffering of any kind is ongoing, however, the need to weep periodically is also ongoing. Golda Meir expressed this beautifully when she wrote: "Those who do not know how to weep with their whole heart don't know how to laugh either." Weeping is cleansing, healing, comforting and a way of releasing tension, sorrow, frustration, anger and loneliness. Like laughter, it is an important language of the soul.

When my friend sat with me that day, I felt as if her words gave me permission to cry—and the tears began sliding down my face. Within minutes, however, I felt guilty. "I'm feeling sorry for myself," I thought, and that was not acceptable, because I'd come to a place where I felt strong and courageous in living with my illness the best I could. To me, "brave" had come to mean "not crying." Even though I knew better, I had unconsciously equated being tough with being brave.

I had a lot of thinking and sorting out to do that summer. I would walk to the church a block from our house, where I could sit alone in the dim, comforting light, facing the altar and the flickering red and blue votive lights. There I would listen to the velvety night sounds and the creak of the ceiling, sounds that became familiar to me, like friendly voices. Because the nights were warm, I would turn on the electric fan and let the air gently blow my hair, as if I were catching a breeze fresh off the surface of the ocean. I would feel myself slowly melting into the pew as my thoughts stilled, easing and erasing the suffering of the day. When I would step back out into the starry summer night, I would feel like a cloak of gladness had been draped over my shoulders.

With time, I realized that I have a similar place within, a place where I can feel sorry for myself in a way that is soft, accepting and embracing—a place where I can sob. There, in that inner place, a sense of peace washes over me as I feel a deep kindness for myself and others.

I will always remember that summer as the season when I learned to weep with all my heart.

Weeping Jesus, thank you for understanding that sometimes tears should not be hastily dried but rather encouraged to streak down our faces and drip off our chins. Our tears are prayer at its most powerful.

Flying

*If I take the wings of the morning
and settle at the farthest limits of the sea,
even there your hand shall lead me,
and your right hand shall hold me fast.*

Psalm 139:9-10

I was standing at the sink washing my hair when a memory came to me that I hadn't thought of for over twenty years. It was 1976 and my dad was dying of cancer. I was in my early twenties at the time and had absolutely no experience with terminal illness. Dad did not look that sick to me. When I visited him, he would sit quietly, not talking much—just as he always did. I vastly underestimated how sick and weak he was because it did not show.

"Hey, Dad," I said to him one afternoon. "Come over to Grandma's house with me and help me remove the oak stairway railing. I need it for my house." Grandma's old house stood empty, and I wanted the railing for my own house that was being remodeled.

Dad's response was subdued. "I don't think I can," he said.

"Oh, come on, Dad," I chided. "You've been sitting all week. It will be good for you to move around."

As Dad rose—without a word of protest—and followed me across the yard to Grandma's house, I chattered happily about all my dreams and plans, envisioning the railing on my own staircase. Dad began to tire, however, as soon as we started our chore. His face paled and became white, his breath became shallow, and cold sweat began dripping off his face. Even now, I remember how stunned I was. "Joni," he whispered weakly, "I can't do this." Shock filled me as I observed the level of suffering he was going through— and felt the crushing guilt of not having understood.

As a child, I had a recurring dream that I could fly. It was a marvelous and freeing dream, the stuff of a Peter Pan childhood. After Dad died, however, I never had that dream again. Washing my hair at the sink that day, I realized that my child-like belief in magic and innocence died along with Dad. Now, when I think of my dad's noble spirit—his willingness to help me when he knew he couldn't hold up and the immediate for-giveness he had for a daughter who could not under-stand—I feel a deep warmth within, knowing that he would not want me to feel bad about what happened. If he could, Dad would reach down to me through time.

This bittersweet experience taught me how invisible serious illness can sometimes be. Suffering does not always show. As I travel my own complicated journey with chronic illness, I recall the blue sky and white clouds in those childhood dreams of flying and imagine what it would have been like to view the beauty of the world from a bird's eye view high above the ground.

God of My Father, we all need warmth and flight. The older we get, the more profoundly we understand.

Death Mask

While I kept silence, my body wasted away....
You are a hiding place for me.

Psalm 32:3, 7

The ambience was perfect: good friends, animated conversation, lavender-scented candlelight, diamond lights sparkling from my miniature Christmas tree, wine, cheese and crackers. I'd been anticipating this gathering all week. Everything was perfect, except for one thing. Some days, I am weaker than others—and this was one of my weaker days. No amount of rest seemed to turn the symptoms around. Often, because I am so eager to see my friends, adrenaline kicks in and I can recover enough to hold up for a while. Not this time, however. After ten minutes, I had to admit, "I can't talk."

I'll never forget how traumatic that night was for me. I was horrified at how my body could fail me in such a major way. I kept wanting to cry, "This is not the real me! This is not fair!" I was mortified that my friends had to see me like that. "We wish we could do something for you," they said, obviously frustrated in their own helplessness. We all felt powerless about the situation. I thought, "How can I expect anyone to go through this with me? It is too much to ask."

The next day, my friends called one another to discuss the dilemma—then they called me. They wanted to know what dreams I had and how they could help make them come true. I felt enveloped by their care and gradually began to feel more secure in being vulnerable with them. It was a process for all of us as we learned to become familiar with the framework of my illness and its limitations. Time, commitment, sensitivity and the respect they had for my journey helped me find myself again.

The most mystifying element for my friends and relatives to understand has been my need for space. When I don't feel well, I sometimes don't like to talk on the telephone or see people, because coping requires all of my resources. I simply cannot converse, because my limited resources are depleted by illness. I have often wished that I could run to those who love me and say, "I still care and always will—even when you don't hear from me."

That festive holiday night, as I sat feeling overwhelmed while my friends spoke gently with one another by candlelight, a gift memory had come to me. I found myself reliving a mystical experience I had many years before, when I had taken Christian clown ministry training at a retreat. I envisioned myself staring into a mirror, white clown paint smeared all over my face. This is called the death mask, the one applied before putting on the celebration colors that uniquely bring your clown character to life. As I sat applying that white death mask all those years ago, I was mesmerized by the sight of my face disappearing, until all that remained were my eyes. They appeared like brilliant blue coals, so transparent that I felt as if God were gazing back at me from the mirror, looking directly into my own eyes.

Applying the death mask is considered a solemn ritual, during which one is not to speak because it would diminish the sacredness of the transformation. I got through that disappointing party by remembering how right it can feel to honor the sacrifice of not speaking.

God of Clowns and Silent Joy, when we are too ill to talk, there is another way to look at it. Not speaking is not always a limitation.

Acceptance

"Arise...and come away;
for now the winter is past."
Song of Solomon 2:10-11

Once again, the limitations of my illness had escalated, ruining an important event that I had been
looking forward to. I was heartbroken and ready to call
it quits, muffled by a blanket of sorrow. I had really had
it.

It had snowed off and on that entire week, but
not enough for anyone to notice. That was how I felt
inside: snowing a little. When I looked out over the back
yard, it appeared as if someone had shaken a huge
sack of flour and lightly dusted the whole village. I, too,
felt dusted by suffering and stress.

I struggled, trying to resist the limitations that kept
presenting themselves to me, until one day I couldn't do
it anymore. The energy just wasn't there. The surprising
thing was that by accepting the limitations I finally
found my voice. By realizing I couldn't have it all or be it
all, I found a path. I began to view God as my mooring.

After spending the morning with my thoughts

and a pot of hot tea, I was reminded that intuition and instinct reveal God's voice to me. I remembered that I am not a solo pilgrim in the realm of suffering but a fellow traveler of many who—like me—seek fullness, discovery, bravery and a deep passion for life, truth and God. I found courage in acceptance.

For me, acceptance does not mean saying "yes" to suffering or giving it permission to stay. Rather, acceptance means not fighting something that refuses to be fought. It means not beating myself up emotionally when answers and healing don't come in the way I or others would like. Acceptance means nurturing and taking care of myself, sinking into and loving people who are there for me, and being there for them. It means a redefining of hope, not grasping at every straw but nestling down with common sense, having the intelligence to know when a shift in thinking is required. Acceptance means recognizing when it is time to let go of certain expectations and create new ones.

God of Winter, acceptance carries within it the gift of peace and renewal. Like the promise of spring, it warms the soul deep within, even before the season of thaw begins.

The Christmas Hush

S ometimes we have experiences that are magical. When we get old, we will want to gather children around us so that we can recount our stories of these magical experiences. When night falls and wind rattles the door, this is the tale I will tell by the glow of candlelight:

Once upon a time, years ago on a Christmas Eve, I was very sick—so sick that I couldn't go with my husband and sons to Grandma's house to celebrate Christmas and open presents. Instead, I sat alone by our Christmas tree and thought—mostly about nothing in particular.

Time lapsed as I sat there and listened to the clock: tick-tock-tick-tock. It was nearly 6:00 p.m. As evening shadows deepened, the tiny white lights on the tree seemed to come alive in the growing darkness. Beyond the window, dusk had arrived.

I suddenly felt an urgency to go out doors. A good friend of mine, who was in his eighties at the time, once told me about a phenomenon that he called the Christmas Hush. He said that he had experienced it long ago, when he was the storekeeper in our town during the Thirties. To my friend, the Christmas Hush was like a mantle that dropped over the town only once a year, on Christmas Eve. All would be still and pure with an expectant ambience.

I was afraid that if I stayed in the house that Christmas Eve, I would miss the Christmas Hush. Determined, I dressed warmly, got some sliced apples from the kitchen, and focused on my destination: I would go to see the horses across the road and meet the Christmas Hush there with these friends.

Although the path was extremely icy, the evening air was invigorating. The snow squeaked under foot. I paused at the end of our driveway, gazing up town at empty Main Street—not a car in sight. I imagined my friend leaning out the door of his store all those years ago, marveling at the Christmas Hush, the light from his store spilling out onto the snowy sidewalk while the fragrance of his wife's oyster stew drifted down from upstairs.

By then, my legs were starting to tremble, but the longing to be out in the night outweighed the voice in me that said, "You need to be in bed." I could see the four horses in the barnyard, less than a block away. I made the short trek to the wooden fence and leaned on it, calling to them.

They didn't seem to be in any hurry to see me. Rather, they stared calmly while I laughed, feeling familiar with their ways. One finally clopped over, thrusting his dinosaur-sized head as close to me as possible. I gave him a good scratch while he nuzzled at my pockets. Eventually, his partner joined us and politely dipped her nose over the fence for a friendly pat, too. I took my gloves off so my friends could muzzle the apples from my bare palms. While the mare ate one, the male gobbled three pieces, chomping noisily. Looking for more, he gave me a hearty nudge, and I was struck by the beauty of his deep chocolate-colored eyes, dramatic against his white coat. Standing there in the snow, clinging to the wooden fence for support, a warm feeling came over me. I knew it was the mantle of the Christmas Hush.

I knew, too, that I would never experience a Christmas like that again. As I made the trek home, I pondered the powerful beauty in a horse's familiar gaze, the profoundness of a deserted street, and the sacred kinship that can exist between all God's creatures and people who, like my storekeeper friend, share the same roots.

Christmas God of Times Forgotten, the hush of your presence in the world is always there, just waiting for us to stop and notice.

The Strand Gatherer

I will let you find me, says the Lord...and
gather you from all the nations.

Jeremiah 29:14

Times of awe should not be rare, because they come
in response to God's revelation—God, who is always
at work, parting inner stage curtains, expanding our
vision, and revealing secrets and truths that we didn't
know before. A long time ago, I embarked on a vision
quest—a spiritual undertaking that spanned years.
When I look back, I can almost imagine curtains rising as
I sit in the dark, watching my inner journey unfold as if on
a stage.

In the opening scene, I see myself in a hospital
going through dark days, where words, medication and
people cannot reach me. Then the scene changes, as
if with a sweep of the hand, to a landscape not unlike
Ezekiel's valley of dry bones—a place barren and vi-
cious, with sandstorms blinding and burying me.

Suddenly the scenery changes again. The dark
becomes even blacker and a single spotlight illuminates
the worst night. I experience a time unlike any I've had

before or since. Suffering has me in its jaws, and I feel like I have reached the breaking point of not being able to bear it.

Then a young girl comes to me, like a voice within, yet separate. This young girl—my eternal, strong and ageless self—says to me, "You can do this, Joni. You are strong. You are healing." Her words become like a mantra that will carry me through long and terrifying nights.

With time, the mysteries I was experiencing deepen, and the imaginary curtains rise on another scene. I sit with a letter from a close friend resting in my lap. Following heartache and illness, I had written to her asking, "What is my place in life? What is my work?" She had written in response, "You are called to gather strands." I remember feeling a light go on in me as I read my friend's simple yet profound words.

Then, once again, the scene changes. The stage is suddenly bathed in beautifully colored floodlights and, on the stage, I see a woman twirling amidst bones, her arms flung wide, her long hair flying. As she twirls, she gathers thousands of silver and gold strands that swirl about her and out into the universe.

I shared these scenes and my sense of grief concerning my health limitations with another friend, an artist. She responded, "It's as if your body, held back, held down, sends your spirit, imagination and creativity flying, searching, soaring into the invisible sources of energy that connect and enliven us all." She told me about a tall, empty canvas that was waiting for her, affirming my feeling that we are all empty canvases with many possibilities waiting to happen, no matter our age, life circumstances or health.

Time passed. One day, my artist friend was sitting in a concert listening to Bach. As the music swelled about her, she began sketching. A beautiful, dancing woman emerged, catching in her hands thousands of swirling strands that coupled with the universe. The sketch became a painting, "The Strand Gatherer," an image that inspired and now graces the cover of this book. To me, the Strand Gatherer personifies the resilient human spirit, gathering the strands of possibilities, mystery, healing, safety, strength, creativity, freedom, faith, justice and unity within us.

Strand Gatherer God, when we feel as if the curtain has dropped and we are alone in the dark, help us gather hope.

Something White

He was transfigured before them...and his clothes became dazzling white.

Matthew 17:2

N ight was fading to a cold, white, winter dawn. New-fallen snow dusted our wooden deck and, deep in the woods, I could see the horse-sleigh road, visible through the black, shadowed trees. Sometimes the mysterious paths in our lives become so visible and apparent that we feel as if Something White—like the snow that morning—has descended to mark the way through dark passages.

My friend sat across from me in the living room as dusk fell later that afternoon, a candle flickering nearby on my grandmother's trunk. We had been estranged, my friend and I—the chasm between us widening as the years rushed by. "We've been afraid to trust each other," I offered as an explanation. She nodded in agreement. As we spoke, it felt as if Something White drifted down upon us, gentle yet more powerful than the rift. We had both recently experienced sorrow and suffering, and caring had brought us together, as we each offered the first, cautious words: "I'm sorry this has happened to you."

When I awoke the next morning, I watched the faint light strengthen as the new day arrived. I looked at the clock, knowing my friend was on her way to the airport to fly home, back to her own life—knowing, too, that it would be a long time before we saw each other again. My mind traveled over the past, through the years of our separation. I quickly moved through those silent withdrawn years, because they felt like ashes that could be swept away as a new era beckoned us to a renewed friendship.

We all have broken bones in our souls that need mending. When two people come together after being disconnected, the new beginning feels like an unfolding of wings, like a miracle taking place. When we feel as if we have broken bones in our soul and reveal that brokenness to a loved one by saying, "I hurt here. This is a place where the bone got shattered," it's like touching the place, validating the hurt, and giving it permission to mend.

It was snowing as I checked the clock again, knowing that my friend's plane was in the air, her flight carrying her home. Within myself, I sent her a message: "Let's believe in Something White forever. Let's always believe in healing broken bones and leaving ashes behind." In my mind, I blew her a kiss.

Dazzling White Mother God, you are the Something White that mends our shattered places.

Finding Flight

"Is not God high in the heavens?
See the highest stars, how lofty they are!"

Job 22:12

I had a dream about flying kites with a group of close friends—although in reality I had never met the people. The kites were the rich, primary colors of a young child's set of large, easy-to-hold crayons. In the dream I could feel the string slip coolly through my fingers as my kite went higher and higher, silhouetted against an evening sky. Flying my kite required little effort as I watched it dip and soar. My friends nearby, however, had trouble flying their kites, which kept hurtling and crashing to the ground. When they asked me for help, I simply tossed their kites into the air and they took flight, soaring and dancing on the wind. With the satisfaction that comes with helping others, I handed the kite strings back to my friends and said, "It's not too hard, once you get the hang of it."

Not long after the dream, I experienced a serious misunderstanding with some medical personnel. Because I had grown to depend upon and trust these people, a profound sadness enveloped me. Just prior to this incident, I had been thinking about the power of hope and how people are brought into our lives for a reason. When I became enmeshed in this unexpected, tumultuous conflict, however, that idea seemed to become ridiculous.

I once copied a quote that said, "The peace of God is more than an absence of conflict." Through this hurtful incident I realized how fragile and illusory the feelings of peace and security can be. The images in my "finding flight" dream, however, reminded me to keep my hope alive regarding others and myself, despite the fact that I had to learn to trust in a new way.

As time, the healer of all wounds, carried me like an enduring wind uplifting a kite, I found peace and personal closure when I blessed and let go of the persons involved in the conflict. One of the most hurtful things that had ever happened to me turned out to be a pivotal learning experience. Ultimately, as my kite dream portrayed, when we begin to heal and our sense of inner soaring is restored, we realize that helping others find flight is more important than flying our own kites.

Soaring God, we appreciate the beauty of spiritual flight so much more having been earthbound by heavy cords of mistrust. Those who heal and let go fly higher than they ever dreamed possible. Could it be that the deeper the wounds, the higher we can soar?

Gypsy Woman

Who is that coming up from the wilderness,
leaning upon her beloved?

Song of Solomon 8:5

For a long time I have harbored the fallacy that suffering or trial is supposed to make me gentle. However, I have not been able to attain the archetype of who I thought I should be (or become) as a person with serious illness. I have carried this incomplete paragon I call the Suffering Woman for many years, always trying to measure up to her—and falling short. I really wanted this illness to make me gentle. I wanted to become the perfect Suffering Woman, transformed without protest into grace, holiness and style.

The truth is, illness or trial does not make us gentle. Rather, it makes us authentic. Falseness is done away with in the trenches of pain. When the inner battles of chronic illness are waged, the journey is about soul survival.

I sometimes let my mind go wild, creating images that strengthen me. The other day I found myself imagining a woman with dark, piercing eyes: the Gypsy

Woman. She wears gold chains at her throat, ankles and wrists, and they all jingle with intriguing, meaningful charms. Her sturdy boots are of aged leather, and her well-worn clothes are of magnificent jewel colors—deep purple, scarlet and emerald green. Her blouse is cut low, revealing healthy flesh, and she has an ageless look about her that is impossible to determine. Her graying hair is wavy and unruly, held back by a comb of black pearls.

This time, the Gypsy Woman is on a significant journey, driving a covered wagon pulled by a white horse with blue tassels dangling on his bridle. Storm clouds gather in the sky, and the horse shakes his head as thunder rumbles in the distance. The Gypsy Woman calls robustly to the horse, her hands firm but affection-ate on the reins. A small, secluded ravine is just ahead, and they pull into it to rest for the night.

After watering and vigorously rubbing down the horse, the woman retires to her wagon. It is like a small cabin and contains many wondrous things. She winds a music box with a monkey on top, smiling to herself at the familiar melody. Lighting a small, beaded lantern that illuminates fringed draperies, she sets about prepar-ing a light supper of mulberries and dried fish. Two yellow canaries perch nearby, while a miniature dog laps the milk she sets out for him. The wind picks up and rocks the wagon, but storms are nothing new to the Gypsy Woman and her companions. "We'll ride this one out, like always," she says, as she steps out of her lovely clothes, draping them on nearby pegs.

In the dim light, the Gypsy Woman applies a healing salve to several tender, new scars on her body, telling her loyal dog, "They will heal as thoroughly as the old scars." Her eyes cloud momentarily as a fierceness sweeps her countenance.

Before she slips between coverlets of fragrant, sun-drenched cotton, the Gypsy Woman opens a small skylight at the top of the wagon so that she can see the stars come out after the storm. Her prayers are honest, to the point, and strong—offered to the God she knows and loves well. There is a sound like voices whispering as the overhead leaves of the sheltering tree brush against the wagon top. Dark clouds obscure the moon, but as the Gypsy Woman catches a glimpse of it through her porthole, she says matter of factly, to no one in particular, "I spit at suffering."

When my daydream ended, I wrote it down— then laughed at what I had written, feeling immensely pleased.

Robust God, thank you for laughing with us while the wild images of our imagination bring us strength.

Annie's Story

My people will abide in a peaceful habitation,
in secure dwellings, and in quiet resting places.
Isaiah 32:18

A common misconception held by the general public is that those of us confined to our homes by serious chronic illness feel trapped or held captive. When I first became ill and someone said that my house was like a cage, I was deeply saddened. The fact is, I love our home. In some ways, it has been my salvation.

Decades ago I named our house Annie. To me, the name sounds friendly, warm and unpretentious. Annie has quite a story. She was once a country church, like the ones you see on Christmas cards. When my husband and I purchased the building, she had stood empty for nearly ten years. Although waist-high weeds surrounded her and most of her frosted cathedral windows had been shot out, I fell in love with Annie the moment I laid eyes on her. Debris, piles of leaves, and dead rabbits littered her basement, but when I stepped through the swinging wooden doors of her nave, the perfect tin-sculpted ceiling, wooden floors and quiet, shadowed spirit of the place enfolded me.

The years have flown by. As a house, Annie has been transformed and grown, just as our family has. Now, nearly two and a half decades later, she has come into her own...as have I. There won't be many more physical or exterior changes in Annie. Rather, she will experience a progressive deepening that will continue to reveal her true nature in subtle ways. There is now lace at her windows and black and rose Victorian carpeting spanning her living room, small studio, two sets of stairs, and upper loft. Three amber, gold, moss-green and plum stained-glass windows filter the warm afternoon sun.

Annie is saturated with our family's joys, heartaches and dreams. She is our ship that creaks when winter winds blast her outer walls. She has bats in her tower every spring, and she shelters us through the storms of life. My friends say that coming here is like having a shawl dropped over their shoulders or a cool drink offered when life is overheated and the road dusty and long.

I think it must have been a curiosity to Annie when safety bars, railings and a handicap ramp had to be built for me when I got sick. Yet these things did not diminish the dignity of either Annie or me. A house may be just a building to outsiders looking in and, sadly, a cage to some—but to me, my house is a sanctuary...a world within a world.

Divine Consoler, overshadow this quiet resting place, this dwelling set apart for healing, loving and living. Let purity of heart flourish here.

In Highest Honor

I have called you by name, you are mine....
You are precious in my sight,
and honored, and I love you.

Isaiah 43:1, 4

To me, the word "fragile" does not mean "weak." Rather, "fragile" refers to an element of the deepest deep that should be noted with mindfulness, sensitivity and respect. Because of my upbringing and cultural conditioning, it has taken me decades to realize that experiencing vulnerability is not something to be ashamed of, apologized for, or taken as a sign of character weakness.

I have a Comfort Box (my Box of Spring) that I created for myself one winter. In it are fragile trinkets, old photographs and jewelry, a beaded purse, carved wooden animals, and many more treasures with meaning to me. The mummified body of a hummingbird also lies nestled in the bottom of my Comfort Box. Perfect in every detail, I consider that hummingbird to be one of my most sacred treasures. It came to us one summer, when one of my sons found it lying dead in our garage.

Native people consider hummingbird feathers to be magical, having the perceived power to "open the heart." The medicine of hummingbird feathers is considered fragile, their mission joy. Those who live with serious struggles know how fragile hope can be; suffering can make us feel imprisoned, despite our greatest efforts to rise above it.

The hummingbird represents the loss of important things I have had to let go of. It inspires me to feel compassion for those who have felt the passion of their faith wither away. It reminds me that there is an ancient magic in the universe, that God does indeed keep watch over us when we are suffering.

Gossamer God and Guardian of Delicate Things, thank you for holding and honoring our fragile hearts—our deepest fears and thoughts—in your Box of Spring.

Grandma's Way

*Lord, you have been our dwelling place
in all generations.*

Psalm 90:1

My beloved grandma always planted a large
garden. She had a row of blue bachelor's but-
tons along the wire fence, and I remember how dozens
of white butterflies always flitted among the cabbages.
In the winter, Grandma would dump ashes from her
cast-iron cook stove into the garden, and then in the
spring, she would work the ashes into the soil with a hoe.

Grandma always worked in the garden in a
cotton housedress, a calico apron, and a wide-
brimmed straw hat that came to a point and tied under
her chin. She was one of my best friends, and I tagged
along with her like a small shadow, pestering her wher-
ever she went, whether she was hanging clothes on the
line, making homemade soap in the shade behind the
house, getting the mail, or separating cream in the milk
house. She liked having me around; we shared a kinship. All was right with the world when I was around
Grandma, which was practically all the time, since Mom

and Dad's little house was right next door to her and Grandpa's big house.

Grandma was steeped in her life on the farm— the rich soil she worked, the grapes she picked by the creek and made into jelly, and the yellow, swooping finches (which she called "canaries") in the grove that she marveled at. There was a spirit of merriment about Grandma that was quiet and uncomplicated. You could sense it in her clear, spectacled eyes, which I always said were as deep as a lake, and in her easy laughter that was just below the surface. She worked hard, rose early, listened to religion on the radio, and loved me. She made neat hats out of folded newspaper for my sister and me to parade around in, and she talked Norwegian on the telephone. The only time I heard her raise her voice was when she called the cows.

Grandma knew what it was like to endure cold winters of the soul. Her mother died young and, as the oldest girl, Grandma raised her five sisters and one brother while nurturing her heartbroken father. Years later, when her husband developed Parkinson's disease and became slower with each passing year, she took care of him, too.

Grandma was a woman of the land. Its rhythms and seasons ran in her blood, and that was her legacy to me. I feel her strength stir within when winter visits my own soul. It is proper—and an honor to Grandma—for me to think about growing things in the dead of winter, whether it be faith or flowers. When illness feels like it is getting the best of me, I remember the roots and sturdy heritage I come from. I recall Grandma's weathered, sun-drenched skin, her worn, capable hands that pulled bee stingers out of me more than once, and her way of going about her business. Grandma lived with purpose. She paid attention to her world and was plugged into something enduring. She always had time to express wonder or to sit down with a child to share a sugar cookie and cherry-flavored Kool-Aid. She waded knee-deep in the tides of life, reminding her granddaughter, even decades after her death, that there are dimensions within us that hardship and illness can't touch.

God of Gardens and Grandmas, never let us forget how soul-filling the feel of warm earth trickling through our fingers can be—how sacred it is to be a child of the land.

A Visit to Church

Comfort, O comfort my people....
The uneven ground shall become level,
and the rough places a plain.

Isaiah 40:1, 4

Sometimes it takes all our inner resources to cope with illnesses. If we are troubled or worried about something, our ability to cope with our illness is seriously affected.

A bad memory had been haunting me for several days. I should say "again," because it was one that would sneak in every once in a while when I was tired, stressed or worn out. That memory had nagged me the entire weekend, making me feel vulnerable and upset. Finally, on Sunday afternoon, I said, "Enough is enough."

I put on my coat, scarf and gloves, grabbed my cane, and went outdoors. I was weaker than usual, and it took an act of will to force myself beyond the mailbox. "I can't do this," I thought. But my other voice said, "Oh, yes, you can!" I needed to walk, breathe fresh air, and sit by myself in church. Even though that meant walking a block from my house, I was determined.

Although it had snowed the night before, I noticed that clear, dry spots were already appearing on the gravel road, dry enough to walk on securely. It occurred to me that healing is like that. The strong places in the soul surface early, creating level avenues that one can journey on, even if there is a lot of area that still needs melting and healing.

It took a little fortitude, but I gradually made my way to church. The snow on the steps hadn't been shoveled off, so I gripped the railing and plodded my way up to the front doors, leaving footprints in the snow behind me. They reminded me of all the tracks and progress I had made spiritually during the past difficult year. Where once my whole heart had felt like one large chunk of ice, there was now only a tiny "ice chip" remaining that I couldn't seem to get rid of no matter how much time, prayer and inner work I put in.

When I stepped inside the church, I was greeted by old, familiar smells that had been a part of my life for several decades: floor wax, wood polish and the occasional whiff of old incense. The double doors swung closed behind me, and I made my way to the front of the church. I sat in a pew where our oldest son had carved a tiny dinosaur when he was little, catching my breath, gazing at the large, bare, rough-hewn cross that had been set up for Lent. The atmosphere was stark and imposing, bringing serious thoughts. I looked up at the curved, cedar boards of the ceiling that always remind me of Noah's ark. Of everything in our church, I love the ceiling best. It has an enduring, simple beauty about it. While I reflected, the ice chip in my wounded heart pierced me like a thorn, reminding me of its presence and why I had come.

Pierced God of Sorrows and Triumphs, help us to live with a large heart. Send gifts of inner forbearance, compassion and the healing of memory. Help us to sink to the "underneath" strong places in the soul that, like the surface of the gravel road peeking through the melting snow, are level and secure places upon which we can walk.

Woman at the Well

The woman said to him, "Sir, you have no bucket, and the well is deep. Where do you get that living water?"

John 4:11

Years ago I faced a season in my life that called for tremendous healing following complicated surgery. Convalescing at my aunt and uncle's lakeside home, I spent hours writing in my journal. Over and over I wrote the same thing: I felt like I had been thrust into a deep well and that it would take an act of God for me to find enough strength to sit in a chair. Day after day, week after week, I wrote, "Still in the well. Still in the well."

Looking out the large picture window to the nearby lake, I would experience the strong spirit of place that the lake evoked. I would lie in my room at night knowing that its moonlit presence was just yards away, summoning me like a friend even while I slept. When I left that place two weeks later, I sadly said goodbye to my lake friend, watching it recede in the distance through the car window. I had never been able to go down to it, not even once; I simply did not have the strength. I felt as if my life energy had been completely drained, my body serving as the framework of a well gone dry.

When I first became ill, the life-giving water that I longed for at the soul level, represented by the lake, seemed just out of reach. For me, the lake's energy and beauty symbolized the vitality that illness was draining from me. Although I tried to make sense of my illness in those early days—to find a spiritual stronghold—the disjointed words I wrote in my journal clearly indicate that I was given no revelation.

Today, I wish I could go back and offer comfort and encouragement to the person I was in those days. I would say, "Don't try so hard, relax. Put away your pen and unfold and heal gently. Let go of the desire for meaning and mindfulness when your body is simply too sick to function."

Well-Spring God, let us taste your living water. No matter how mindless and feeble illness might make us, we long for the waters of your peace.

Revealers of the Heart

May the Lord direct your hearts to the love of God.

2 Thessalonians 3:5

When my health deteriorated, I found myself on a path of evolution that cried out for expression. I found the use of imagery to be a lifeline, opening up a whole new world for me. Studying archetypes became especially intriguing.

An archetype is a symbolic personification of the psyche, such as the wisdom of the Old Woman—one of the most widespread archetypal personifications in the world. My journey with chronic illness and pain takes shape when I consider the archetypal women within me.

For example, I once imagined a woman covered with scars. I did not find her ugly, however, merely herself. There was an ancient knowing about her, and I felt as if I wanted to protect her. In my imagination, I stayed with the image and watched the woman as her outer, physical framework fell away like a snakeskin and a new woman rose up out of her scars. It was like Scar

Woman and New Woman were joined, yet each remained her unique self.

Shortly after I imagined New Woman emerging from Scar Woman, another significant image came to me. This woman came in not one but three images, all involving a bridge. At first I saw her with her arms outstretched, embracing and holding a bridge across her ample breast. Then I saw her arms and hands become the bridge that she extended across a chasm. Following that I saw her lay her entire body across the chasm as the bridge itself. Both people and animals could use her body to cross the chasm safely. I call her Bridge Woman. To me, she represents the world's need for those human beings who are willing to deepen, transform and heal their lives, thereby becoming places of safe passage across chasms of spiritual, political and personal strife.

I have begun to see my life as an ongoing mosaic of images, experiences and encounters that reveal to me my own transformation. When I first began this soul work, Victim Woman was all I had. She was real to me, and her struggle was my struggle. I loved her first. As she was joined by Bone Woman, Wild Woman, Scar Woman, New Woman, Gypsy Woman, Well Woman, Strand Gatherer, and Bridge Woman, however, I loved and embraced them as well. Psychologists would call these images archetypes; scoffers would call them figments of the imagination. To me they are simply Revealers of the Heart.

God of Tender Revelations, only you could transform Victim Woman into Bridge Woman.

River Faith

I am about to do a new thing;
now it springs forth, do you not perceive it?
I will make a way in the wilderness
and rivers in the desert.

Isaiah 43:19

A boggy, odorous rivulet, about two feet wide and only inches deep, zigzags through the center of the woods in the valley below our house. Its pitch-black color and twisted shape are dramatic against the white background of new-fallen snow. After meandering through the woods, Snake Stream, as I call this trickle, wears itself out and flows into Clear Creek. From there, Clear Creek weaves briefly through a fetching spot of woodland where it splashes into Redwood River at a place the locals call The Mouth.

There was a time when I compared my life to Snake Stream: muddy, hidden in the deep woods of my psyche, and trickling through the meanderings of my illness. Then one day the word "connection" became part of my vocabulary. It was like a "something new" that arrived after nearly a year of some of the deepest soul searching I've ever done. I had to "connect" what seemed to be disjointed experiences to reach a new beginning, but once there, I found a serenity I hadn't known before. I realized that I was finding my own power again, which—like the indwelling of God—had been there all along. It was as if the stream of illness in my life, just like the murky Snake Stream, had connected to the refreshing current of Clear Creek, invigorating me with an energy to not only tell my story but to keep doing my inner work for the sake of others as well as myself.

When I stand at my secret spots along Clear Creek and gaze into the water, I am mesmerized by the pace of the current. It moves along with such purpose, as if it is being drawn to the river and nothing can stop it. Even when Clear Creak is at its lowest, in the summer, it shimmers over shallow, pebbled shoals reflecting the sun in an intriguing play of light all the way down to the bedrock. Snake Stream does not exhibit this merriment. Rather, it wanders with little purpose, barely sliding over mud and threading through dark places untouched by sunlight. While Snake Stream speaks to me spiritually of the dark night of the soul, I know that it flows toward a point of connection with light and life.

Suffering carries a potential that can empower authentic faith and hope. It is when we are suffering that we can best understand that divine consolation courses through the marrow of our heartaches, where we need it most. Pain inspires us to want to live for others, to move beyond our own miseries, and to fall in love with God and our own lives.

The connecting of the three waters—Snake Stream, Clear Creek and Redwood River—symbolizes for me the journey of suffering. Snake Stream embodies the narrow, harsh times we all experience. Eventually, however, Snake Stream connects to Clear Creek, that gentle but relentless call within each of us to keep flowing through the transforming waters of sorrowful experiences until we join a more powerful current. Finally we arrive at a place like The Mouth, where Clear Creek connects to and is engulfed by Redwood River. Our suffering may not go away, of course, but there is a "downstream" feel to it that connects us to a deeper trust that we can hang on to and that hangs on to us. We cling to that trust, knowing that—no matter what happens—we won't be destroyed.

God of Mighty Rivers and Murky Streams, when suffering causes us to feel like a muddy puddle of anguish, carry us gently—from one connection to the next—to that deep, clear place of trust within.

Move On

O ne day our youngest son, not quite thirteen at the time, decided to clean his room—a rare event. I could hear him making a lot of racket and when I went to investigate I discovered that he had moved all his young, boyhood stuff out into the hallway. Grinning, he said that he was "half a man, now" and that he didn't want "baby" stuff in his room anymore. Stricken, I stared at his stuffed animals, cowboy hat, storybooks, Halloween clown costume, bucket of Leggo building blocks, and first pair of ice skates—all haphazardly piled in the hallway. While it was no big deal to him, his discarding and moving beyond his childhood things was extremely poignant to me. I lamented, "You can't grow up. You're my last little boy!" He said, "Ah, Ma, I'll always be your little boy."

Several years later I made a rite of passage myself. I had run out of storage space in my dressing room and bedroom, and the clutter was causing me to feel cluttered inside. I'd put off addressing this project because it felt too overwhelming. Finally, inspired and helped by our middle son—a renowned organizer—I went through boxes, dresser drawers and closets, filling a dozen large garbage bags with old clothes. I was ruthless. I decided to throw out or give away anything that hadn't been worn in recent years. Out went all my old bathing suits (some going back nearly twenty years), never-worn bath robes, wool suits, outdated dresses, shoes, a winter coat, and a pink vinyl rain jacket from the Seventies.

Each item had memories attached to it like a price tag. I remembered how I felt when I wore the items and who I was at that period in my life. For example, there were the dresses I wore to our sons' confirmations and high school graduations, and the outfits I'd worn to my brother's wedding and my mom's and father-in-law's funerals. Going through the old clothes was like going through a scrapbook of my life. I actually felt teary eyed as I touched the clothes for the last time. They represented many seasons in my life—joys, sorrows and everything in between.

I stuck to my guns, though, and very little was spared. Later, when my youngest son and I were watching television together and he lay sprawled across the sofa sucking a freeze pop, I said, "Hey Mic, remember the time you threw out all your old stuff because you weren't a little kid anymore?"

He said, "Yep."

"Well, I just threw out all my old clothes, too, from when I was young."

"Well, that happens," he said. "Move on."

With that simple comment from a boy without guile, I consciously made my rite of passage from being a young woman to a middle-aged woman, from being a well person to one who is learning to cope with chronic illness. I had empty drawers and lots of space in which to reinvent and redefine my life.

Awesome God of Order and Simplicity, you nod in approval and say, "Too much clutter, no room for the soul."

Spangles of Light

The light of the sun will be sevenfold, like the light of seven days, on the day when the Lord binds up the injuries of his people, and heals the wounds.

Isaiah 30:26

One Easter morning I awoke through a haze of dreams just as the sun was rising. I was in that twilight state—partially awake but still mostly asleep—curled up, facing east. The sliding glass doors in our tower room framed the tops of the trees as if they were artfully arranged in a shadow box. Through my half-opened eyelids, I sensed a powerful light shining on my face. It was the Easter sunrise, floating up through the dark woods in a gigantic disc of glowing white light.

Despite the heaviness of slumber, I kept watching the sky, remaining caught in a spell. It was a low, dark, somber sky that created a horizontal ceiling across the tops of the trees. When the fiery sun reached it, the ceiling of the sky pressed down and became a barrier to the light. In response, the sun seemed to flatten at the top and bulge at the sides, forcing the light to expand at a phenomenal rate. Spangles of light blazed out from beneath the clouds and streaked across the heavens and through the woods. Caught between the dream world and wakefulness, I realized a magical thing was occurring. A silent laughter of pure white seemed to fill my beloved woods all the way to its roots.

I then fell into a deep sleep. Later, when I got up, a sense of wonder embraced me throughout the day, as if the finger of a divine experience had lightly touched me. I have never seen a sunrise like that before—or since. I know in my heart that I witnessed something glorious and out of the ordinary that Easter morning.

The experience reminded me that God not only changes shape to fit our souls' framework but also permeates the places in us that are lowest, darkest and the most needy. That spectacular Easter sunrise spoke deeply to me about the struggles of chronic illness. It taught me that when the dark ceiling of suffering stretches heavily over our souls, God's light and encouragement simply spangles out from beneath.

God of Easter Spangles, sometimes we need to believe in miracles. Thank you for not letting us down. Because of you, we believe in those spangles of light that embrace us with Easter wonder and hope.

Proverbs for Life

The Teacher also taught the people knowledge,
weighing and studying and arranging many
proverbs.... He wrote words of truth plainly.

Ecclesiates 12:9, 10

Many years ago while attending a retreat, I was
asked to write the legacy I would like to leave
my children and loved ones. I have updated and
changed it through the years, but below is my legacy.

Be gentle with others. Don't expect them to think
or believe exactly as you do, because they won't. You'll
only be disappointed and disillusioned if you set unreal-
istic expectations of others.

Remember that there is a gray side to almost
every black and white issue; in other words, things are
never as cut and dried as you might think they are.

If you put your life or other people's lives in molds
or boxes and think you know all the answers, you are in
for a tremendous fall. Don't short-change yourself;
always make room for new thoughts and the people
who bring them.

Never allow yourself to grow bitter; it will ruin your health and drive away your most loyal friends. Don't be so easy on yourself that you grow soft, but always be patient with yourself. Honor the processes at work within you. Always set realistic personal goals so that you have something to work for and look forward to. Feeling disappointed about who you wish you could be or repeatedly regretting things you can't change is a waste of time. Do your best and leave it at that.

A good way to help those who are searching for wholeness is to keep reminding them that they have worth. Tell loved ones how special they are. Be stingy with advice. Nudge but never preach. Always remind yourself to build up others, no matter what your own limitations are. In doing so you build up yourself.

Strive to maintain the personal maturity that allows you to see beyond yourself. You can measure your inner growth by the tolerance you have for others who rub you the wrong way. Guard your mouth and weigh your words.

Expect to make mistakes. When you go through an inner tempest, don't trust your feelings. Nothing can create false perspectives better than out-of-control emotions. Beware of making decisions when you are lacking a calm spirit, because you will more than likely regret it later.

Recognize the times when stress is destroying your hope. Regroup and gather back that which saves you. Your instincts will tell you what you need to know and do.

Don't start new projects or inner seasons without finishing the ones at hand, lest you grow discouraged without the gratification of completion or closure.

Pay attention to the circumstances, messages and people who come into your life.

Take inner discernment seriously, and always follow the threads of it. Understand that the subtle is as much an element of God's voice as is the dramatic.

In the end, you will find that life is a process of three things: believing in yourself, believing in others, and believing in God. Realize that it is your privilege and responsibility to be true to the unfolding. When hardship and suffering come, delve as deeply as you can into the vast inner universe of resources that lies beneath the struggle. Trust that the sacredness within you will hold you up. Breathe it, pray it, embrace it. Let go, expand and float.

Teacher God of Lessons Learned, help us to be quick learners, to not keep repeating the same mistakes or patterns that prevent us from growing and trusting.

A Dream

Everything old has passed away; see, every-thing has become new!

2 Corinthians 5:17

I had risen unusually early that day because I wanted to develop an idea on my computer. I worked passionately most of the morning, but by mid-afternoon, I couldn't hold up; my energy was draining. I collapsed gratefully into bed and fell immediately into a deep, exhausted sleep. I had a dream that afternoon, so vivid that I remember it as if it had been an event that actually occurred.

I dreamed that I was sitting at the table in my studio, chatting with a counselor friend. As we talked, I felt a weakness come over me. This happened several times, making it difficult for me to hold up my head. In the dream, I became so tired that I rested my head on the table and, just like that, I died.

My friend jumped up from the table in alarm and reached toward me. I wanted to say, "Don't worry, I'm just slipping away," but I was already gone. Although gripped by death, I felt energized in a calm, comfortable way. As my friend reached for me, a "being" reached through him and lifted me right out of my body. In the dream, I was above it all—watching, feeling safe, unafraid and happy to be free of suffering.

I interpret the dream to mean that I am changing, that a new season is upon me. I have been doing a lot of inner work, as these essays represent. The dream represents the fruit of this labor: the completion of one phase of my life and the beginning of another.

The dream had a serene quality to it that is hard to express. It left me feeling hopeful, with a promise of things to come. Perhaps it was given to me as a gift for doing this work, to let me see that it is possible to experience inner, personal transformation on a sacred level, and that we can be spiritually lifted out of suffering and struggle.

Divine Lifter of Sorrows, you are always creating, bringing new life. Perhaps transforming us when we suffer is your greatest passion. You are so good at it!

Names of God

Healing God of Support and Hope

God of Changing Seasons

God of Hope against Hope

Stalwart God of the Ages

God of Stone and Sky

Parent God

God of Many Faces

Dear Mindful God

God of Inner Doorways

Enchanting God of Trees That Sway
    When There's No Wind

Wholesome God and Ship of Truest Feelings

God of Safe Passages

Faithful God

God of True Hermits and Contemplatives

God of Precious Jewels and Toads

God of Living Stillness

Tenderhearted God of Fallen Trees
    and Bare-Branched People

Gentle God

God of All That Howls

God Who Breathes Life into All Living Things

Weeping Jesus

God of My Father

God of Clowns and Silent Joy

God of Winter

Christmas God of Times Forgotten

Strand Gatherer God

Dazzling White Mother God

Soaring God

Robust God

Divine Consoler

Gossamer God and Guardian of Delicate Things

God of Gardens and Grandmas

Pierced God of Sorrows and Triumphs

Well-Spring God

God of Tender Revelations

God of Mighty Rivers and Murky Streams

Awesome God of Order and Simplicity

God of Easter Spangles

Teacher God of Lessons Learned

Divine Lifter of Sorrows

Acknowledgments

I extend heartfelt thanks to the following professional people and organizations who encouraged both the book and me as we unfolded through many stages:

Don Gadow, Winona University

Mary Southard, CSJ, LaGrange Ministry of the Arts

Linda Smith, HealthEast Foundation

Julie Arvold, Director of Medisota

Michael M. Paparella, MD

The Wabasso Standard

Art Winter, founder and editor of *Praying* Magazine

Rich Heffern, editor at *Praying* Magazine

Pat Samples, editor of *The Phoenix*

Ardis Cloutier, OSF, director of Stauros U.S.A.

Brian Boersma, LICSW

Frances Placentra

Sandy Jenniges

Melanie Schei,

Melanie Dunlap, FNP,

Jamie Tuohy, OTR

I also thank my many friends and relatives who cared and encouraged me throughout the years, standing by me, waiting with grace and understanding when I need to journey alone. You are all diamonds to me.

Finally, thanks beyond words goes to my life partner, best friend and husband, Jerry, for his undying perseverance, and to our three sons, Damian, Dana, Dana's girlfriend, Jennifer Wendler, and Dominic.

Additional Resources for Spiritual Growth

Protect Us from All Anxiety
Meditations for the Depressed
William Burke, with drawings by Mary Southard, CSJ

This best-seller is written in the same format as *Tall in Spirit* and offers help to both people suffering from serious depression and those who live or work with them. Written by a priest of the Archdiocese of Chicago who suffers from depression himself, this unique book offers spiritual and personal insights into coping with the disease.(112 page paperback, $9.95)

From Grief to Grace
Images for Overcoming Sadness and Loss
Helen R. Lambin

A collection of images that assist people in naming, processing and overcoming grief caused by illness, a loved one's death, a job loss or similar difficult situations. (96 page paperback, $8.95)

A Promise of Presence
Weekly Reflections and Daily Prayer Activities
Bridget Mary Meehan and Regina M. Oliver

Fifty-two reflections on the belief that God's infinite presence permeates all of creation while seeking an intimate, personal relationship with each individual. Each reflection is followed by a seven-day prayer guide that provides clear directions for a week of creative, enriching prayer activities. (232 page paperback, $9.95)

The Characters Within
Befriending Your Deepest Emotions
Joy Clough, RSM

Explores the deepest human feelings, fears and motivations. Anguish, Blame, Delight, Exhilaration, Humility, Revenge, Vulnerability, Wonder and 50 other emotions come alive through these whimsical, anthropomorphic, evocative reflections. (160 page paperback, $9.95)

Everyday People, Everyday Grace
Daily Meditations for Busy Christians
George R. Szews

Brief stories of ordinary people experiencing God's grace in their everyday lives, coupled with a carefully chosen scripture quotation for each day of the year. (368 page paperback, $9.95).

Available from booksellers
or call 800-397-2282 in the USA or Canada.

A0004800129928